DELAWARE

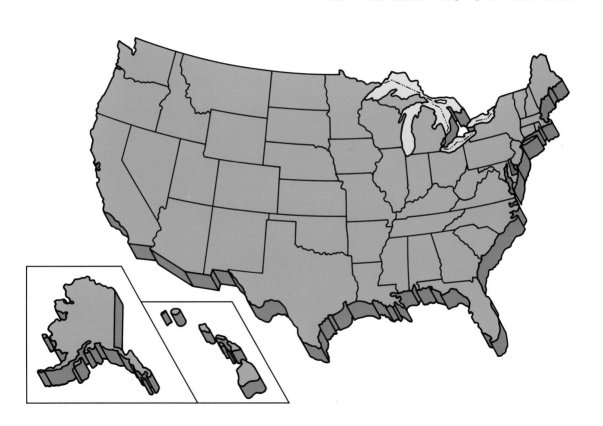

DELAWARE

Dottie Brown

 Lerner Publications Company

LIBRARY OF CONGRESS
CATALOGING-IN-PUBLICATION DATA
Brown, Dottie.
    Delaware / Dottie Brown.
        p.   cm. — (Hello USA)
    Includes index.
    Summary: Introduces the geography, history, and people of Delaware. Includes famous people, state highlights, and current environmental issues.
    ISBN 0-8225-2733-2 (lib. bdg.)
    1. Delaware—Juvenile literature. 2. Delaware—Geography—Juvenile literature. [1. Delaware.]
I. Title. II. Series.
F164.3.B76 1994
975.1—dc20   92-44845
                                            CIP
                                            AC

Manufactured in the United States of America

1 2 3 4 5 6 – I/JR – 99 98 97 96 95 94

Cover photograph by Barbara Laatsch-Hupp / Laatsch-Hupp Photo.

The glossary that begins on page 68 gives definitions of words shown in **bold type** in the text.

CONTENTS

Did You Know . . . ?

❑ Delaware's Dover Air Force Base houses the largest cargo planes in the world. Each one is so big it could carry 48 Cadillacs or 25,844,746 Ping-Pong balls.

❑ Delaware was the first state to join the United States of America.

❑ So many big chemical companies have their headquarters in Wilmington, Delaware, that the city is known as the Chemical Capital of the World.

☐ More bananas are shipped into the United States through Wilmington, Delaware, than through any other port in the country.

☐ Cypress trees—common in the U.S. South—can be found as far north as the Great Cypress Swamp in southern Delaware.

☐ The first log cabins in North America were built in 1638 by Swedish settlers in what is now Delaware.

A Trip Around the State

Blown off course by a fierce storm, British captain Samuel Argall sought shelter in a bay off the Atlantic Ocean in 1610. Before he sailed away, Argall named the bay De La Warr, after the governor of Virginia. Common use shortened the name to Delaware. Soon, Europeans gave the name to the river that feeds the bay and to the Indians who already lived in the area.

Later, Delaware also became the name of a Mid-Atlantic state—the second smallest state in the United States. Pennsylvania borders Delaware to the north, and Maryland forms the state's southern and western boundaries. The Delaware River, Delaware Bay, and the Atlantic Ocean shape the eastern edge of the state. Across the wide Delaware Bay lies New Jersey.

Blue heron

Delaware has two major land regions. The Atlantic Coastal Plain covers almost all of the state. A small semicircle of land called the Piedmont caps the northern tip of the coastal plain.

The soil of the low, flat Atlantic Coastal Plain is sandy. **Marshes** (grassy wetlands) line much of the shore. The Great Cypress Swamp sprawls along Delaware's southern border. This **swamp** (wooded wetland) once covered nearly five times the area it does now, but farmers drained most of it to create some of the state's richest cropland.

Trees rise from the waters of Trussum Pond in southern Delaware.

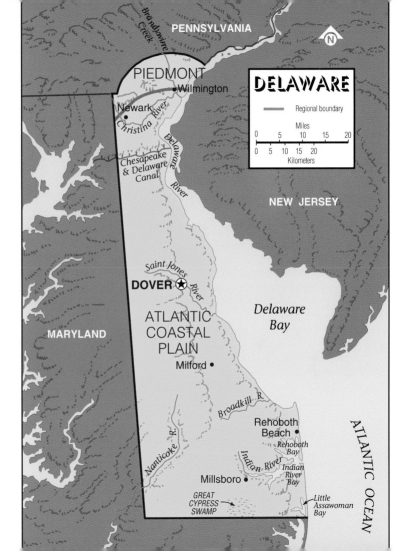

DELAWARE

| Regional boundary |

Miles
0   5   10   15   20

Kilometers
0   5   10   15   20

N

PENNSYLVANIA

Brandywine Creek

PIEDMONT

Wilmington

Newark

Christina River

Chesapeake & Delaware Canal

Delaware River

NEW JERSEY

Saint Jones River

DOVER ★

ATLANTIC COASTAL PLAIN

Milford

Delaware Bay

MARYLAND

Broadkill R.

Rehoboth Beach

Nanticoke R.

Indian River

Rehoboth Bay

Indian River Bay

Millsboro

GREAT CYPRESS SWAMP

Little Assawoman Bay

ATLANTIC OCEAN

Rolling hills cover the Piedmont.

North of the coastal plain, hilly farmland blankets much of the Piedmont. A thin layer of clay soil coats the thick, hard rock that lies underneath. Although the Piedmont stretches only 10 miles (16 kilometers) at its widest point, it is home to roughly two out of three Delawareans. Most of these people live in or near Wilmington, the state's largest city.

Delaware has many rivers. Its largest and most important river, the Delaware, flows southward into Delaware Bay. Other chief waterways include the Christina River and Brandywine Creek, both of which empty into the Delaware River. The Broadkill, Indian, and Saint Jones rivers cross southeastern Delaware, flowing into Delaware Bay. In southern Delaware, the Nanticoke River travels westward into Maryland.

Ships from around the world sail into Delaware Bay, heading for inland markets along the Delaware River. Three small bays—Rehoboth, Indian River, and Little Assawoman—lie behind long sandbars in southern Delaware. The sandbars have become some of Delaware's most popular beaches.

Canoeists glide down the Delaware River.

13

These beaches—and the sandy soil of the Atlantic Coastal Plain—provide clues to the history of the state's land. For millions of years, most of Delaware lay deep beneath the waters of the Atlantic Ocean. Porpoises, hammerhead sharks, foot-long oysters, and other sea creatures were among the region's few living beings. Gradually, the water retreated from the land, leaving behind layers of dirt, sand, clay, gravel, and other tiny pieces of rock.

Fossils of sea creatures can be found in Delaware's sandy soil, which was once covered by the Atlantic Ocean.

The Atlantic Ocean still affects Delaware. Hurricanes and other severe ocean storms occasionally strike Delaware's coast. Powerful winds rip apart homes, uproot trees, and blast sand off the beaches. The winds also whip the ocean into giant waves that flood the coast.

But most of the year, Delaware's weather is mild. Summer temperatures average 76° F (24° C), and winter temperatures hover around 35° F (2° C). **Precipitation** (rain and melted snow) is plentiful in the state, averaging 45 inches (114 centimeters) a year. Although winters are fairly warm, Delaware still gets about 16 inches (41 cm) of snow each year. Most of the snow falls in the north.

Because of Delaware's warm climate, many different kinds of plants thrive in the state. Stands of hickory, holly, oak, pine, and beech trees cover about one-third of the state. Cypress and red cedar trees tower above Delaware's swamps, where rare orchids also bloom. Many flowering trees and bushes, including fragrant magnolias, wild cherries, and tulip trees, blossom throughout the state.

Tulip tree (below)

Holly tree (above)
Hickory tree (right)

16

Water lilies float lazily on ponds and lakes.

Lots of different animals make their homes in Delaware. Deer and mink scamper through the forests. Otters glide through the state's many streams and rivers, while muskrats creep along the swamps. Wading birds such as herons and ibis nest in wetlands along Delaware Bay. On the seacoast, crabs, clams, and oysters hide in the sand.

White-tailed deer (left)
River otter (above)

Delaware's Story

In 1967 a real-life detective story unfolded in a field along Delaware's coast. Scientists there dug up an ancient burial site that held 90 graves. With clues from stones, bones, shells, and pieces of pottery, the scientists worked to solve the puzzle about who was buried there. They discovered that the graves belonged to American Indians, or Native Americans, who had lived in the area between 1,000 and 1,500 years ago.

These Indians were among the first known people in what is now Delaware. They hunted deer, elks, beavers, and foxes for food. They fished, and they dug clams and oysters from the seashore. The Indians also gathered seashells to decorate clothing. Prized for their beauty, some of the shells were traded to other Indians as far away as the Mississippi River.

No one knows for sure what happened to Delaware's first people. They were gone by the time European explorers arrived in the area in the 1600s. But a different nation, or tribe, called the Lenape was living near the Delaware River and Bay.

According to Lenape legend, the world was built on the back of a giant turtle. Men and women sprouted from trees that grew on the turtle's back.

By carefully digging through the soil, these boys hope to uncover objects that may give clues to Delaware's past.

The Lenape, whom the Europeans called the Delaware, were a peaceful people. Like the Nanticoke, their neighbors at the southern end of Delaware Bay, the Lenape lived along rivers and streams in villages of 50 to 200 people. On the outskirts of the villages, the Indians grew corn, squash, and beans. Beyond the crops were hunting grounds.

Each Indian family lived in its own dome-shaped wigwam, which was built with tree limbs, bark, and grass. The women wove baskets, sewed clothing from animal skins, tended the children, planted crops, and cooked meals. The men fished and carved dugout canoes to travel by water. They also hunted deer, beavers, and other animals.

The Lenape fished by stretching wooden fences across streams. When fish passed between a set of fences, the Indians stood ready to spear them. The catch was then smoke-dried and stored for winter.

Twice a year, the entire village journeyed inland to hunt. As they walked, the men were ready to defend their families from danger. The women carried the belongings. Sometimes when the villagers reached a thick grove of trees and shrubs, they set it on fire to drive out animals for easier hunting.

Though the Lenape were peaceful, the powerful Susquehannocks frequently attacked them. The Susquehannocks, who lived to the north and west, killed so many Lenape that many of the survivors fled their homelands. The Susquehannocks also attacked the Nanticoke.

Meanwhile, another threat to the Indians arrived. In 1609 explorer Henry Hudson sailed into Delaware Bay while looking for a route to Asia. Hudson quickly realized he was heading the wrong way and sailed back out the next day. But his short visit was the first of many European voyages to the area. The Europeans would change the Indians' way of life forever.

Hudson worked for the Dutch government, which soon claimed the land around the Delaware River and built a **colony**, or settlement, at Swanendael. The Dutch traded European goods for furs with the Lenape and made money by selling the furs in Europe.

In 1638 Swedish settlers bought land from the Lenape and built Fort

In 1631 a group of Dutch settlers landed near what is now Lewes, Delaware.

Christina in what is now northern Delaware. The Swedes had heard that the area had rich farmland and good fishing. Like the Dutch, the Swedes came to make money.

Misunderstanding at Swanendael

In 1631 a group of about 30 Dutchmen landed at what is now Lewes, Delaware. So many swans swam in the marshes there that the Dutch named the area Swanendael, or Valley of Swans. Swanendael was the first colony in what is now Delaware.

The newcomers quickly constructed some brick buildings and began to clear land for planting crops. The settlers made friends with the local Lenape, and they traded food and drink with each other. The two groups got along well until a misunderstanding arose over a painted shield of tin hanging outside the Dutch fort.

To the Dutch, the shield was a coat of arms, a symbol of their country that commanded honor and respect. To the Lenape, it was simply an object they had never seen before.

Curious about the shiny metal object, one of the Indians took the Dutch coat of arms. The Dutch got very angry. Before long, the Indian who had taken the tin shield was found dead. One version of the story says the Dutch killed the Indian. Another account claims the Lenape killed him to keep peace with the Dutch. Either way, the Lenape later decided to get even for the death of their friend by killing all of the Dutch colonists at Swanendael.

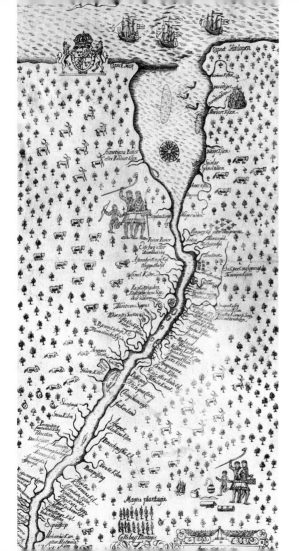

Settlements built by the Swedes extended far up the Delaware River. They named the area New Sweden.

The Swedes' fort stood on a river they named the Christina in honor of their country's 12-year-old queen. Inside the fort's sturdy walls, the Swedes built the first log cabins in North America. The settlers quickly went to work planting rye, pumpkins, cucumbers, turnips, and watermelons. By the 1650s, nearly 400 settlers lived in New Sweden, the first permanent European settlement in what is now Delaware.

The Dutch worried that the Swedes might try to make money in the fur trade, too. So the Dutch sent warships up the Christina River and claimed New Sweden.

But the Dutch soon lost New Sweden to the British. In 1681 William Penn founded the large British colony of Pennsylvania to the north. Penn needed a route to the sea, so he took control of coastal lands in the region now called Delaware.

Penn divided Delaware into three counties—New Castle, Kent, and Sussex. Together they became known as the Three Lower Counties because they were south of Pennsylvania. As the colony's governor, Penn allowed the Three Lower Counties to make their own laws, which gave the colonists a great deal of freedom.

North of the Three Lower Counties, Philadelphia quickly became an important center of trade and the fastest growing town in Pennsylvania. Farms sprang up along the rivers and streams of New Castle because it was closer to Philadelphia than Kent and Sussex were. Farmers shipped wheat, rye, barley, and corn up the Delaware River to be sold in Philadelphia.

A model of a flour mill shows the different stages of grinding grain into flour.

Wilmington, in New Castle County, became a thriving town on Brandywine Creek. The stream's swiftly flowing water was used to power mills that ground wheat into flour. Flour from the Brandywine mills was famous for how white and finely ground it was.

As more and more Europeans moved into the Three Lower Counties, the Native Americans of the region lost land they had depended on for hunting and farming. Many Indians also died from diseases they caught from the Europeans. To escape these problems, the

Lenape kept moving farther west. By the mid-1700s, all the Lenape had left the Three Lower Counties. Many Nanticoke also had left.

At about the same time, Great Britain was at war with France, fighting for control of the North American fur trade. The British wanted the colonists in Pennsylvania and other North American colonies to help pay for the war. So the British government passed a series of laws forcing the colonists to pay taxes on tea, glass, paper, and other items that came from Britain.

Colonists in the Three Lower Counties were part of Pennsylvania, but they had their own paper money.

The colonists were angry about the taxes. Many colonists decided they wanted to be free of British rule. By 1776 all 13 British colonies in North America had joined together to fight a war—called the American Revolution—to gain independence from Britain.

Soon after the Three Lower Counties entered the war, they separated from Pennsylvania and united to form the Delaware State. British

Ceasar Rodney was a representative to the colonial government from the Three Lower Counties. He raced through a stormy night to reach Philadelphia in time to cast his vote for independence from Great Britain. A statue in Wilmington honors his ride.

Delaware's troops marched from Dover to fight in the revolutionary war.

troops occupied Delaware for several weeks in 1777 and controlled the Delaware River for eight months.

Many Delawareans fought in the Revolution, helping the colonies win independence from Britain in 1783. Four years later, Delaware became the first state to approve the **constitution** (written laws) of the United States—the country formed by the former colonies. For this reason, Delawareans earned the nickname First Staters.

By 1830 boats called sloops were bustling into Brandywine Creek to deliver wheat from surrounding states. The sloops were reloaded with flour to be shipped to Philadelphia and overseas.

After the war, many businesses thrived in Delaware. Shipyards were built in nearly all the port towns along Delaware's rivers. Shipbuilders crafted wooden sloops, schooners, and fishing boats out of pine and white oak. Paper mills and cloth mills also prospered, and Wilmington continued to grow as a center for flour milling.

Soon the Brandywine Creek's strong current attracted a new kind of miller. In 1801 a wealthy French **immigrant** named Eleuthère Irénée du Pont bought a large stretch of land north of Wilmington. Having learned how to make fine gunpowder in France, du Pont built large powder mills along the Brandywine in 1802. The mills quickly became successful.

At the same time, new crushed-gravel roads called **turnpikes** gave farmers in northern Delaware an easier route to more markets. Farmers could now sell more wool, butter, and other products.

31

Dover's Legislative Hall, where the state's lawmakers meet, is patterned after government buildings from the late 1700s.

Travel by boat improved after steamboats were built in the early 1800s. Ships no longer had to rely on wind to move them through the water. Paddling along Delaware's rivers, steamboats carried passengers, coal, lumber, and gravel in record time.

In 1829 the Chesapeake & Delaware Canal was completed. This water route linked towns along Delaware Bay to important markets on the Chesapeake Bay in Maryland. The canal cut hundreds

The Chesapeake & Delaware Canal sped up shipping from Delaware.

of miles off the route between the two bays.

In the 1830s, Delawareans began laying railroad tracks. The railroads reached into Kent and Sussex counties. For the first time, farmers in southern Delaware had an easy way to get their crops to market. New towns sprang up all along the tracks.

Some of Delaware's farmers owned slaves from Africa, but most of the black people in the state were free. Many Delawareans and people in other Northern states wanted to end slavery entirely.

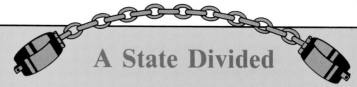

A State Divided

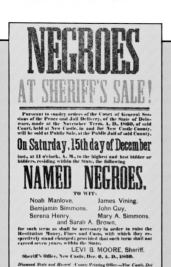

Patty Cannon

The people of Delaware could not agree on whether slavery was right or wrong. The state had some laws that helped African Americans. Other laws worked against them. Slavery was allowed, but in the late 1700s the state passed a law forbidding any new slaves from being brought into Delaware. African Americans were considered free unless they were proven to be slaves, but, like slaves, free blacks were not permitted to enter the state.

Two famous Delawareans, Patty Cannon and Thomas Garrett, held very different opinions about slavery. From the late 1700s until 1829, Cannon led a gang that kidnapped slaves and free blacks and sold them to slave traders. Sometimes Cannon even murdered the slave traders in order to take all of their money. Kidnapping was illegal, but it was murder that finally got Cannon arrested in 1829. She died in jail, while waiting to be hanged.

Thomas Garrett believed slavery was wrong and devoted his life to helping slaves reach freedom. While living in Delaware, he helped about 3,000 escaped slaves reach Pennsylvania, where slavery was not allowed.

Helping slaves escape was illegal in Delaware, and in 1848 Garrett was caught. The judge who heard his case gave him a big fine, and Garrett lost all his property in order to pay it. But the heavy penalty did not stop Garrett. He told the judge that he would still help any slave who came his way.

Thomas Garrett

Southern states, however, depended on unpaid slave labor to earn a profit on **plantations**, or large farms. When Northern states tried to force Southerners to end slavery, several Southern states formed their own country, the Confederate States of America, in 1861.

Soon after, the Civil War broke out between the North and the South. Delaware joined the Union, or Northern, forces. Most of the state's men fought for the Union. But some Delawareans sided with the South.

Du Pont's mills provided more than one-third of the Union's gunpowder. Fort Delaware, on Pea Patch Island in the Delaware River, held Confederate prisoners of war.

After the Union won the war in 1865, slaves throughout the South were freed and black men gained the right to vote. But white Delawareans, worried about the power African Americans might have if they voted, passed a law requiring people to pay a tax before they could vote. Many black men couldn't afford to pay the tax, and tax collectors refused to take money from those who could.

New inventions spurred the growth of industry in the years following the Civil War. In northern Delaware, where most of the state's industry was centered, trains brought in coal and iron ore from Pennsylvania to make steel. Wilmington's factories used the steel to make transportation equipment. Delaware became one of the biggest manufacturers of trolley cars, train cars, and riverboats.

The state's tanneries made expensive leather from animal skins. Mining and construction companies throughout the country bought gunpowder milled in Delaware. The companies needed the gunpowder to blast away layers of rock that covered minerals and to clear paths for building roads.

During World War I (1914–1918), Delaware's shipyards bustled to build ships for the fighting overseas. Gunpowder companies worked day and night. After the war, these companies branched into new areas as their chemists developed dyes, paints, and chemically produced fabrics such as rayon.

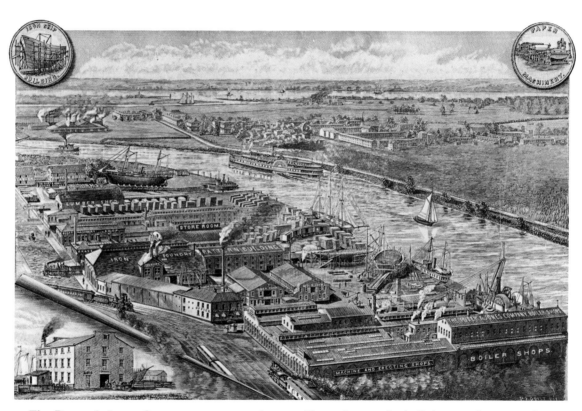

The Pusey & Jones Company was one of several large ironworks in Delaware that turned out ships and other iron products.

The du Ponts

When three young du Pont cousins—Coleman, Alfred, and Pierre—became the Du Pont Company's leaders in 1902, the men quickly turned the Delaware business into one of the largest in the United States. But the family that ran the company was important in other ways, too.

In 1910 Coleman du Pont gave Delaware $4 million to build the nation's first divided highway. The new roadway gave a big boost to the state's economy by providing farms and factories with a fast and easy route to get products to market.

Alfred du Pont took an interest in children and in the elderly. In 1929 he started a plan to give money to old people who could no longer work for a living. And upon his death, Alfred donated much of his fortune to set up an institute for crippled children.

Throughout the early 1900s, Pierre du Pont paid for many new schools for African Americans. He also set up educational standards that all schools had to meet. The large sums of money Pierre donated greatly improved education in the state for both white and African American students.

Alfred

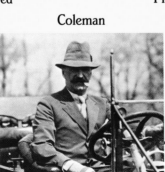

Coleman

Pierre

38

In the plastics department at Du Pont, a worker assembles the nose of a bomber plane during World War II.

In 1939 Du Pont built a new factory in Delaware to make nylon, a fabric used to make parachutes. Orders for nylon poured in during World War II (1939–1945).

After the war, some large companies chose to move to Delaware because laws in the state were friendly to businesses. Delaware's population increased dramatically as these big companies brought many of their workers with them.

The new companies also made more jobs available for white Delawareans. But African Americans did not have as many choices. They could not attend the same schools as white students or go to the same restaurants and theaters. In 1952 Delaware ruled that the separation of blacks and whites in public places was against the law.

White communities were very slow to accept the ruling. Poor housing for black people was one of many issues that led to riots in Wilmington in 1967 and 1968. Delaware's governor called in the National Guard to end the violence.

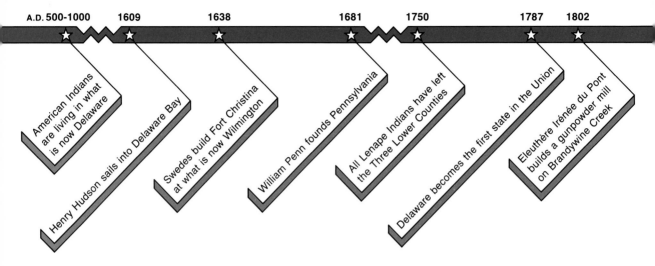

| A.D. 500-1000 | 1609 | 1638 | 1681 | 1750 | 1787 | 1802 |

American Indians are living in what is now Delaware

Henry Hudson sails into Delaware Bay

Swedes build Fort Christina at what is now Wilmington

William Penn founds Pennsylvania

All Lenape Indians have left the Three Lower Counties

Delaware becomes the first state in the Union

Eleuthère Irénée du Pont builds a gunpowder mill on Brandywine Creek

After the riots, the state passed a fair-housing law to make sure African Americans had the same chances as white people to live in decent housing. The state also passed laws to ensure that black students were allowed to attend the same schools as white students. And in 1968 James Sills became the first African American elected to serve on Wilmington's city council.

First Staters know they have accomplished a lot, and they are willing to work hard to achieve more. As a former governor of Delaware once said, "The state that started a nation can also lead a nation."

40

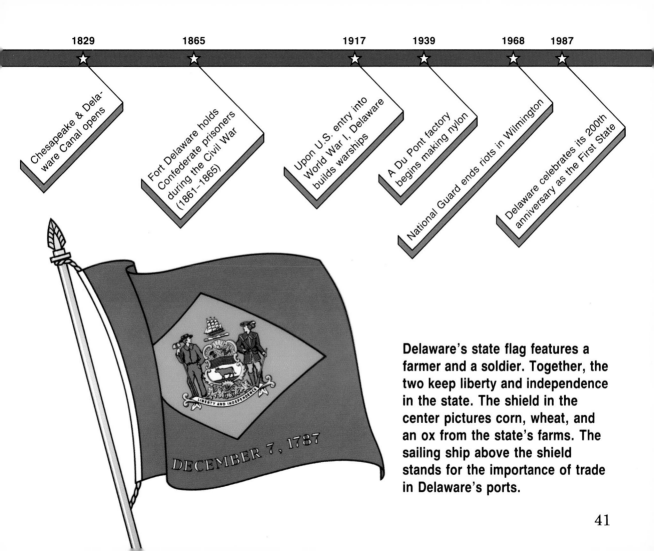

1829 — Chesapeake & Delaware Canal opens

1865 — Fort Delaware holds Confederate prisoners during the Civil War (1861–1865)

1917 — Upon U.S. entry into World War I, Delaware builds warships

1939 — A Du Pont factory begins making nylon

1968 — National Guard ends riots in Wilmington

1987 — Delaware celebrates its 200th anniversary as the First State

Delaware's state flag features a farmer and a soldier. Together, the two keep liberty and independence in the state. The shield in the center pictures corn, wheat, and an ox from the state's farms. The sailing ship above the shield stands for the importance of trade in Delaware's ports.

Living and Working in Delaware

A drive across the longest part of Delaware takes less than three hours, and a trip across the widest part takes less than one. Delaware is the second smallest state in the nation. And, with only about 670,000 people, it has the fifth smallest population in the United States.

Delaware may not be a large state, but it can boast about how much it packs into a small area. For instance, the Nemours mansion is only a short drive from Wilmington. There, visitors can tour Alfred du Pont's French country estate, complete with a château (castle) and formal gardens.

The Nemours garden and mansion *(facing page),* **built in 1910, is patterned after a castle built in France in the 1600s.**

Built 300 years ago, the Old Swedes Church in Wilmington reminds some Delawareans of their Swedish ancestors.

Du Pont's background was French, but many Delawareans are descendants of the state's early Swedish, Dutch, and British colonists. African Americans make up about 14 percent of the state's population. About 500 Indians who are descendants of the Nanticoke still live in Delaware. Small numbers of Asian Americans and **Latinos**, or people from Latin America, also live in the state.

Three-fourths of all Delawareans live in cities, or **urban** areas. Wilmington is Delaware's biggest urban area. On the state's northwestern border lies Newark, Delaware's second largest city. The state capital, Dover, is in central Delaware and ranks as the third largest city.

The Nanticoke Indians in Delaware hold a powwow, or ceremonial gathering, each fall.

Delaware's cities offer many opportunities, including the chance to find out what life was like in another time. At the Henry Francis du Pont Winterthur Museum, people can stroll through more than 100 rooms that display American art and furniture dating as far back as 1640. In Dover, visitors can stand on the very spot where Delawareans voted to approve the U.S. Constitution in 1787, making Delaware the first state.

During the 1800s, children set up for a tea party in this room *(above)* at the Winterthur Museum. Historic buildings and cobblestone streets can be found throughout Delaware. New Castle *(right)* was the state's first capital city.

Throughout the year, festivals draw visitors to Delaware's cities and state parks. Each May on Old Dover Day, many historic homes and buildings in the capital city are open to the public in a celebration of the state's heritage.

That same month, Milford hosts the World Weakfish Tournament, where First Staters try to catch a fish whose mouth is so weak that lifting it from the water by a hook will tear it. In the fall, the Nanticoke Indians hold a two-day powwow in Millsboro, where they perform ceremonial dances, tell stories, and demonstrate Indian crafts.

Throughout the summer months, sun and surf lovers flock to southern Delaware's Rehoboth Beach, one of the state's most popular recreation sites. The beach has even been nicknamed the Nation's Summer Capital because so many visitors come from Washington, D.C. The nation's capital city, Washington, D.C., is about 125 miles (201 km) west of Rehoboth Beach.

The calm waters of Rehoboth Bay make it a popular place for sailing.

47

Outdoor enthusiasts also can hike in Delaware's state parks, bike from inn to inn along the seashore, or try their luck at catching tuna, shark, and marlin in the Atlantic Ocean. And the excitement of

Horses gallop to the finish line at the Winterthur Point-to-Point race.

squealing tires and fast cars lures fans to Dover Downs International Speedway.

When First Staters are not playing, they work in a variety of jobs. Many of Delaware's workers provide services such as selling homes, repairing automobiles, and flying airplanes. Other types of service jobs include waiting tables, selling clothing, teaching students, and driving trucks. More Delawareans have service jobs than any other type of work.

About one-fourth of the money Delaware earns comes from manufacturing goods. Chemical products such as medicines, plastics, paints, nylon, and special materials used for space travel are among the most important items First Staters make. The state also ranks as one of the nation's leading automakers.

Delaware's workers prepare several types of food, too. Some people cook puddings, can pickles, or make soft drinks. Others process fish or pluck and package chickens. Still others bake desserts, breads, and pastries.

Delaware's location on the ocean makes shipping an important service industry.

Although only 3 out of every 100 Delawareans work in agriculture, farms cover about half the state. Huge poultry farms in the south raise millions of broilers, or young chickens—Delaware's most valuable farm product. The sale of broilers earns Delaware more than $400 million each year. Dairy farms in central and northern Delaware produce about $18 million worth of milk each year.

Some farmers in the state grow soybeans and corn, Delaware's most important crops. Most of the soybeans and corn are used to make feed for broilers. Other big crops include barley, wheat, peas, and potatoes. Apples are the largest fruit crop.

Delawareans gather a harvest

from the sea, too. Each year workers in the fishing industry catch more than $2 million worth of crabs, clams, oysters, lobsters, sea bass, and weakfish.

With so many crops and products, and with so much to see and do, First Staters can boast about many things. Delaware may be a small state, but it makes a big contribution to the nation.

Seagulls hover around a fishing boat off Delaware's coast.

Protecting the Environment

Delaware's rivers and bays have long been important, providing transportation, food, jobs, and recreation for the people who live in the state. But these waters are in trouble. As Delaware has grown, factories, farms, and people have polluted its waterways.

With its wide opening, Delaware Bay can rely on a fresh supply of ocean water to flush out many pollutants. But to the south, three inland bays—Rehoboth, Indian River, and Little Assawoman—share only one small opening to the ocean. As a result, pollution in the three bays collects much faster than it can flow out of them. The buildup of pollution has started a chain of events that could destroy much of the bays' wildlife and could close popular beaches.

Pollution in the inland bays is one example of **nonpoint pollution**, which can't be pinpointed to just one place. Much of the nonpoint pollution comes from southern Delaware's many farms.

Bathed in sunlight, a fisher *(right)* reels in his line on Silver Lake in Rehoboth Bay. Muskrats *(inset)* and other animals feed on plants along the shore.

If too much pollution backs up in Delaware's inland bays, people will have to find other beaches to play on.

For example, farmers use chemicals called pesticides to kill insect pests. Farmers also use fertilizers to help crops grow. Fertilizers contain nutrients, which help nourish plants. Sometimes manure is used as a natural fertilizer. But in addition to nutrients, manure also contains bacteria, or germs that can cause disease. When farmers apply too much fertilizer and pesticide to their fields, rain washes away the bacteria, the chemicals, and the excess nutrients. Rain also washes away loose soil.

Dead broilers from the state's many poultry farms also produce bacteria. Some of the birds die of natural causes and cannot be sold for their meat, so they are buried. As the broilers decay, bacteria forms and pollutes the soil. This bacteria also gets washed away during rainstorms.

Rainwater that carries pollutants such as bacteria, chemicals, nutrients, and loose soil is called **runoff**.

Rain quickly washes soil and fertilizer from bare fields into waterways.

The runoff flows into streams that empty into the bays, where the pollutants change the natural order of life in the water.

55

For example, nutrients feed rootless water plants called algae. But with so many excess nutrients from runoff, too many algae then grow on the surface of the water. Eventually, the algae die. In the process, they use up oxygen that fish need to survive.

Thick mats of algae block sunlight from the plants at the bottom of the bays, killing the plants and leaving fish and shellfish with less food.

Scientists adjust a meter that reads how fast the water is moving in Indian River Bay. The speed of the water tells how fast pollution travels through the bay.

Pollution in the inland bays endangers the lives of shellfish such as the horseshoe crab *(above)*. In all of the state's bays, shellfish populations sometimes drop so low that shellfishing is banned *(above right)*.

Bacteria and chemicals from the runoff are eaten by fish and other sea creatures. When they consume these pollutants, fish and shellfish become unsafe for people to eat. High levels of bacteria also can make swimmers sick.

Many Delawareans realize that nonpoint pollution is a serious problem. Farmers and state officials are working together to solve it. Before applying fertilizer

Some farmers spread manure on their fields to fertilize crops.

to their crops, farmers can test the soil to see how much fertilizer they need to grow healthy crops. Farmers then can adjust their machines to spread just the right amount of fertilizer.

Farmers are taking other steps to prevent runoff, too. Instead of plowing up crops after each harvest, many farmers now leave crop stubble on the ground and plant through it in the spring. The plant cover helps hold the soil and nutrients in place.

To help reduce the spread of bacteria, Delaware encourages poultry farmers not to bury dead broilers. Instead, farmers can place birds in dead-bird composters. By layering straw and manure along with the dead birds, farmers can trap enough heat in the composter to make the birds decay quickly. In just a couple of months, farmers then have a heap of compost, or very fertile soil, to use on their fields.

Dead chickens can be composted in large bins to help control the spread of bacteria.

The thousands of water birds *(facing page)* that feed on Delaware's shores depend on clean water.

At the University of Delaware's annual Coast Day, visitors can see and touch sea creatures and learn why it's important to keep waterways clean.

Delaware's state officials and businesspeople are working to educate other Delawareans about nonpoint pollution, too. For example, industries give free education kits to teachers so schoolchildren can learn about pollution and how to prevent it.

Together, Delawareans are learning how to tackle nonpoint pollution. By cooperating to reduce pollution, First Staters can ensure a clean and healthy future for their inland bays.

Delaware's Famous People

Felix Darley (1822–1888), a popular illustrator, moved to Claymont, Delaware, in 1859 He illustrated *Rip Van Winkle, The Legend of Sleepy Hollow,* and many other works by well-known authors.

Howard Pyle (1853–1911), born in Wilmington, painted colonial scenes and worked as an illustrator and art teacher. He wrote and illustrated 15 children's books, including *The Story of Jack Ballister's Fortunes, The Merry Adventures of Robin Hood,* and *Modern Aladdin.*

▲ FELIX DARLEY

HOWARD PYLE ▶

RICHARD ALLEN ▶

◀ JAY SAUNDERS REDDING

EDUCATIONAL & RELIGIOUS LEADERS

Richard Allen (1760–1831) was born into slavery and grew up on a plantation near Dover. After buying his freedom, he founded the Free African Society and the African Methodist Episcopal Church. The new church became a stop along the Underground Railroad, a network of secret passages for escaped slaves heading North to freedom.

Jay Saunders Redding (1906–1988) wrote about what life was like for African Americans in *No Day of Triumph* and *On Being Black in America.* Redding also helped found the field of African American studies and taught at several of the nation's finest universities, including Hampton Institute and Cornell. Redding was a native of Washington, Delaware.

JOHN CLAYTON ▶

◀ JOHN BASSETT
MOORE

John M. Clayton (1796–1856) served numerous terms in the U.S. Senate and was secretary of state under President Zachary Taylor. Born in Dagsboro, Delaware, Clayton also served as chief justice of Delaware's supreme court.

John Bassett Moore (1860–1947), a noted lawyer born in Smyrna, Delaware, was widely respected for his understanding of international law. Moore was one of the first judges appointed to the World Court.

Annie Jump Cannon (1863–1941) was born in Dover. Cannon was the first astronomer to prove that nearly all stars can be grouped according to colors. She discovered five new stars and classified more than 375,000 others during her lifetime.

ANNIE JUMP ▶
CANNON

Wallace Carothers (1896–1937) moved to Delaware in 1928 to work for the Du Pont Company, where he developed nylon. The fabric, which is made from woven fibers created in a laboratory, is very strong and has many uses.

Henry Jay Heimlich (born 1920), a native of Wilmington, developed the Heimlich Maneuver in 1974. Within 12 years, Dr. Heimlich's simple technique, which almost anyone can use, had saved more than 10,000 people from choking to death.

HENRY ▲
HEIMLICH

Edward Robinson Squibb (1819–1900), a naval surgeon from Wilmington, believed medicines used by the U.S. Navy were so poor that they kept sailors from getting well. He convinced the navy to build its own drug factory. He later went on to start his own company—Squibb Pharmaceuticals.

WALLACE ▶
CAROTHERS

◄ DALLAS
  GREEN

George Dallas Green, Jr. (born 1934), pitched for baseball's Philadelphia Phillies and New York Mets and played football with the Washington Redskins. Later, Green managed the Phillies, leading them to a 1980 World Series victory. Green is from Newport, Delaware.

Christopher Short (born 1937), a native of Milford, Delaware, pitched for the Philadelphia Phillies from 1959 to 1972. Known as the greatest left-hander in Phillies' history, Short had four different seasons in which he won 17 or more games.

Randy Lee White (born 1953) won All-American honors as a fullback and a linebacker at Thomas McKean High School in Wilmington. From 1975 to 1988, White played defensive tackle for the Dallas Cowboys. Known as the Monster because of his speed, strength, and fierce playing, White made a total of 1,104 tackles in his career.

RANDY
LEE ►
WHITE

◄ JUDGE
  REINHOLD

VALERIE
▼ BERTINELLI

STAGE & FILM STARS

Valerie Bertinelli (born 1960) is an actress who has starred in many movies, including *Aladdin and his Wonderful Lamp*, *C.H.O.M.P.S.*, and *Shattered Vows*. Bertinelli is from Wilmington.

Judge Reinhold (born 1958), an actor born in Wilmington, has starred in several films, including *Ruthless People*, *Vice Versa*, and *Beverly Hills Cop*.

Estelle Taylor (1899–1958), from Wilmington, was a star of silent movies and early sound-track films. She played leading roles in *Don Juan* and in the 1923 production of *The Ten Commandments*.

Kathleen Effie Widdoes (born 1939) has played leading roles in numerous theater productions, including "You Can't Take It with You," "Measure for Measure," and "The Tempest." She also has appeared in movies and television series. Widdoes grew up in Wilmington.

ESTELLE ► TAYLOR

ROBERT
◄ MONTGOMERY
BIRD

HENRY S. ►
CANBY

◄ UPTON
SINCLAIR

WRITERS

Robert Montgomery Bird (1806–1854) was born in New Castle, Delaware. He began his career as a doctor but left medicine to write plays. "The Gladiator" was so popular that it was performed 1,000 times in 22 years. Bird also wrote the novel *Nick of the Woods: or, The Jibbenainosay.*

Henry S. Canby (1878–1961), who taught at Yale University for more than 20 years, was a writer from Wilmington. He is perhaps best remembered as the founder and first editor of the *Saturday Review of Literature.*

John P. Marquand (1893–1960) wrote about wealthy but misguided people living in New England. He won a Pulitzer Prize in 1938 for *The Late George Apley.* Marquand is a native of Wilmington.

Upton Sinclair (1878–1968) was a writer whose work often dealt with social problems. He became famous after his book *The Jungle* exposed the unsafe and unclean working conditions in the meatpacking industry. Sinclair and his family lived in Arden, Delaware, for several years.

Facts-at-a-Glance

Nicknames: First State, Blue Hen State
Song: "Our Delaware"
Motto: Liberty and Independence
Flower: peach blossom
Tree: American holly
Bird: blue hen chicken

Population: 668,168*
Rank in population, nationwide: 46th
Area: 2,489 sq mi (6,446 sq km)
Rank in area, nationwide: 49
Date and ranking of statehood:
    December 7, 1787, the first state
Capital: Dover
Major cities (and populations*):
    Wilmington (71,529), Dover (27,630),
    Newark (25,098), Milford (6,040),
    Elsmere (5,935)
U.S. senators: 2
U.S. representatives: 1
Electoral votes: 3

*1990 census

Places to visit: Wilmington & Western Railroad in Wilmington, Hagley Museum near Greenville, historic houses in Odessa, Bombay Hook National Wildlife Refuge near Smyrna, Dover Downs International Speedway near Dover, Trap Pond State Park near Laurel

Annual events: Delaware Kite Festival in Lewes (Good Friday), Old Dover Day in Dover (May), Watermelon Festival in Laurel (Aug.), Nanticoke Indian Pow-Wow near Oak Orchard (Sept.), Delaware "500" stock car race in Dover (Sept.), Christmas and Candlelight Tours in Brandywine Valley (Dec.)

Natural resources: magnesium, sand and gravel, Brandywine blue granite

Agricultural products: chickens, milk, hogs, soybeans, corn, barley, wheat, potatoes, peas, apples, flowers, shrubs

Manufactured goods: drugs, industrial chemicals, plastics, nylon, gelatin, pudding, packaged chicken, canned vegetables, fish products, soft drinks, cars, paper products

ENDANGERED SPECIES
Mammals—fox squirrel, Delmarva fox squirrel
Birds—bald eagle, brown pelican, curlew sandpiper, tricolored heron, white-winged tern
Amphibians and reptiles—spotted salamander, bog turtle, barking tree frog, northern copperhead
Fish—hickory shad, four-spined stickleback, black-banded sunfish, northern hog sucker
Plants—sugar maple, fly poison, red milkweed, hairy pineweed, slender toothwort, oxeye, scrub oak, spotted phlox

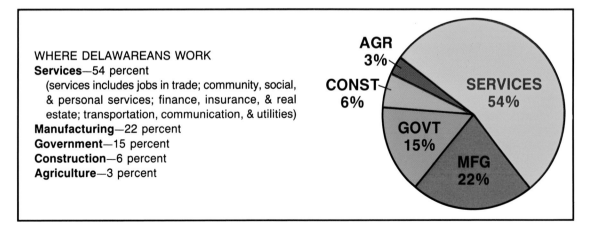

WHERE DELAWAREANS WORK
Services—54 percent
 (services includes jobs in trade; community, social, & personal services; finance, insurance, & real estate; transportation, communication, & utilities)
Manufacturing—22 percent
Government—15 percent
Construction—6 percent
Agriculture—3 percent

AGR
3%
CONST
6%
SERVICES
54%
GOVT
15%
MFG
22%

PRONUNCIATION GUIDE

Assawoman (AS-uh-wum-uhn)

Delaware (DEHL-uh-wehr)

du Pont, **Eleuthère Irénée**
(doo PAHNT, ay-luh-TEHR
ee-ray-NAY)

Lenape (luh-NAH-pay)

Nanticoke (NAN-tih-kohk)

Nemours (nuh-MOOR)

Newark (NOO-urk)

Piedmont (PEED-mahnt)

Rehoboth (rih-HOH-buhth)

Susquehannock (suhs-kwuh-HAN-uhk)

Sussex (SUHS-ihks)

Swanendael (SWAHN-uhn-dayl)

Glossary

colony A territory ruled by a country some distance away.

constitution The system of basic laws or rules of a government, society, or organization. The document in which these laws or rules are written.

immigrant A person who moves into a foreign country and settles there.

Latino A person living in the United States who either came from or has ancestors from Latin America. Latin America includes Mexico and most of Central and South America.

marsh A spongy wetland soaked with water for long periods of time. Marshes are usually treeless; grasses are the main form of vegetation.

nonpoint pollution Pollution coming from a widespread source rather than a specific point. Nonpoint sources of pollution include runoff from fields, pastures, and streets.

plantation A large estate, usually in a warm climate, on which crops are grown by workers who live on the estate. In the past, plantation owners usually used slave labor.

precipitation Rain, snow, and other forms of moisture that fall to earth.

runoff Water from rain, snow, or sprinklers that runs off the land and into streams, lakes, or the ocean. Runoff can carry pollutants from the air and the land.

swamp A wetland permanently soaked with water. Woody plants (shrubs and trees) are the main form of vegetation.

turnpike A highway on which a toll, or fee, is collected from drivers at various points along the route.

urban Having to do with cities and large towns.

69

Index

Acknowledgments:

Maryland Cartographics, Inc., pp. 2, 11; Marc Clery, pp. 2-3, 15, 45, 53 (right); George Karn, p. 6; W. J. Talarowski / NE Stock Photo, pp. 7, 49; Visuals Unlimited: Albert Copley, p. 8, John Cunningham, pp. 14, 50, Leonard Lee Rue III, p. 17 (right), Arthur Morris, p. 51, W. A. Banaszewski, p. 55, Doug Sokell, p. 56 (left); Richard Day, p. 9; Gene Ahrens, pp. 10-11, 12; Jerry Hennen, p. 13; DE Div. of Parks and Recreation, p. 16 (left); Root Resources: © John Kohout, p. 16 (middle), © Kitty Kohout, p. 16 (right), © Alan G. Nelson, p. 53 (inset); John R. Patton, p. 17 (left); William Sauts Netamuxwe Bock, p. 19; Cara Blume, DE DNREC, p. 20; John T. Kraft, Seton Hall University Museum, p. 21; Permanent Collection of the University of Delaware, p. 22; Library of Congress, pp. 24, 35 (bottom); Hagley Museum and Library, pp. 26, 33, 37, 38 (middle & right); Delaware State Archives, pp. 27, 28, 29, 35 (top), 38 (left), 39, 63 (circle); Historical Society of DE, pp. 31, 34; Mae Scanlan, pp. 32, 43; Barbara Laatsch-Hupp / Laatsch-Hupp Photo, p. 42; © 1994 Walter Choroszewski, pp. 44, 46 (right); Winterthur, pp. 46 (left), 48; DE Development Office, p. 47; © 1994 Kevin Fleming, p. 54; Bob Bowden, pp. 56 (right), 57 (right); Lynn Troy Maniscalco, p. 57 (inset); Michael B. Mahaffie, DE DNREC, p. 58; Delmarva Poultry Industries, p. 59; Tracey Bryant, University of DE Sea Grant College Program, p. 60; Jim White, DE Nature Society, pp. 61, 69; *Dictionary of American Portraits,* pp. 62 (upper left, lower right), 63 (upper left & right), 65 (upper left); Delaware Art Museum, Howard Pyle Collection, p. 62 (upper right); Brown University Library, p. 62 (lower left); Heimlich Institute, p. 63 (lower left); Du Pont, p. 63 (bottom); National Baseball Library & Archive, p. 64 (top); Dallas Cowboys, p. 64 (middle); Hollywood Book & Poster, p. 64 (bottom left & right); Museum of Modern Art Film Stills Archive, p. 65 (top right); Yale Picture Collection, Manuscripts & Archives, Yale University Library, p. 65 (middle); National Archives, p. 65 (bottom); Jean Matheny, p. 66; Monica V. Brown, p. 71.